CAUTIONARY TALES

CAUTIONARY TALES

Barbara Goldberg

D DRYAD PRESS
WASHINGTON, D.C. & SAN FRANCISCO

Poems in this book appeared in the following publications:

American Scholar, Antioch Review, Chronicle of Higher Education, Davar, Folio, Journal of Poetry Therapy, Juggler's World, Maariv, Moznayim, New England Review/Breadloaf Quarterly, Ohio Journal, Passages North, Poet Lore, Poetry, Poets On, Salmagundi, Seneca Review, Shirim, Sierra Madre Review, Stone Country, Tendril, Tikkun, Washington Review, West Branch.

Anthology of Magazine Verse & Yearbook of American Poetry (1984, 1985, 1986-87), *Apalachee Quarterly, Finding the Name, Free State, Ghosts of the Holocaust, Hayotzer, Light Year* '86 and '87, *The Chester H. Jones Competition Winners 1983, The Cooke Book: A Seasoning of Poets, The Tie That Binds: Mothers & Sons/ Fathers & Daughters, Whose Woods These Are.*

I wish to thank the National Endowment for the Arts, the Maryland State Arts Council, the Corporation of Yaddo, the Virginia Center for the Creative Arts, and Monica and Gary David for their generous support. Special thanks to Laura Fargas and Elaine Magarrell for their wise insights. *Cautionary Tales* was the recipient of the Camden Poetry Award.

Published by Dryad Press
15 Sherman Avenue
Takoma Park, Maryland 20912

Cover art: *Man Carrying Reluctant Wife,* stencil, 1961, by Pudlo Pudlat. Reproduced with permission of West Baffin Eskimo Co-operative Ltd., Cape Dorset, N.W.T., Canada
Cover design: Paris Pacchione
Typeset at the Writer's Center, Bethesda, Maryland
Printed in the United States of America

Library of Congress Cataloging in Publication Data

Goldberg, Barbara
    Cautionary Tales

I. Title.

PS3557.0355C38   1990   811'.54   89-82737
ISBN 0-931848-78-4

In memory of my father
Eric Heymann

Contents

Cautionary Tales

III

IV

V

CAUTIONARY TALES

In the woods
are these things:

fingers of madmen
nimble and quick
playing cat's cradle
with ropes meant for strangling

a great horned owl
in the treetop
the soul of a Chippewa
caught in its throat

a sidewinding snake
rubbing its scales
jaws unhinged
hungry for neckbones

quicksand, though no one
knows where exactly

These are stories our children tell us
to keep us from wandering.

I

THE WOODCUTTER

The woodcutter's hut
squats in the forest
like a mushroom.

He lives like a monk
and waits for the grim
commands.

He hardly gets to his
chopping. He is given
many tasks:

Once, there was a Queen
who had a hunger
for her daughter's heart.
She called upon the woodcutter
to perform this delicate surgery.

Instead he returned
with the heart of a wild boar,
which the Queen salted,
never tasting the difference.

Again, in the cottage hard
by the edge of the wood
he deftly dissected

a rapacious wolf.
It was as easy as
slicing liver.

A girl and her grandmother
hopped out like little frogs.

At night he comes home
from his labors. His heart
is empty of desire.
He has a simple supper
of bread and cheese.
He hones his ax.

LIKE THE WHALE

*The throat has a small hole and can swallow
an entire household.*
            — Yiddish folk saying

And now in the furnace
of my cavernous belly,
the ancestors set up house.
Mother wants her gilt-edged mirror
in a well-lighted corner.
Father places his knife
and fork at the head
of the table. More people
arrive, the swaggering uncle
in Nazi uniform, he thought
this was a costume party.
The grandfather I never met
discreetly wipes his nose
with his soiled handkerchief.
Swine flu, he murmurs, he feels
a draft. No complaint,
just observation. His wife
scurries about, looking
for unlatched casements. The youngest
soul, the aborted brother
I wasn't supposed to know about,
finds the membranous duct,
climbs up as though it were a beanstalk
and lo! he discovers the tiny hole.
Careful, he whispers, his lips
close to the glottis.
If you treasure us at all,
don't cough.

SURVIVOR

They say I should feed you,
child with the gift of tongues.
But darting through woods of dark pine
hounds chase the scent of sandals.

Days spent under cover
in a field of eiderdown,
my fingers search for traces
of my own lost mother.

At night, when the bulb shines through
the parchment, and I scrub
my body down with soap,
I think of her parting lace curtains
looking for Father to round the corner.

A small patch of pine presses against the North
side of this house. Here, by Union Turnpike,
a car is parked in the driveway.
We'd all fit in, all, if we had
to make a quick journey.
I keep a bar of gold under my pillow.

They bring you to me, my locket
clasped in your fist. I want
to feed you.

It's those spiked needles that scrape
against the glass, those shadows
that won't sleep behind the drapes.
It's that woodsman walking
through this forest
swinging his ax.

TEETH

We all live in dread of our teeth
falling out into our cupped palms.
We pray for our teeth, clattering
in the bone chamber of the skull.
And when the little insanities
creep up from our throat, our teeth,
good soldiers holding their ground,
grind them down in our sleep. And praise
to the wolf with his sharp incisors,
the better to eat. And the ice-maiden's
teeth, sheathed in enamel, biting clean
through the bone. Oh we would never
depart from our eyeteeth, rooted dependably
above our unremarkable necks. And who
is not awed by the white buds of milkteeth
that sprout from red plushness and become
the cutting edge.

HER SOUL TO KEEP

Little girls welcome the beast
to their bed. He shuffles in
to the background song of father
snoring in the old four-poster,
mother baking bread in the kitchen
below, mattress buttons scratched
by little-girl toes. His great
fur face presses the pillow, hot
breath reeking of turnips and
shankbones. Dreams open wide
to the wolf's weight, the pig's
wet snout, that strange white
hoof inside cotton panties.

LES MISÉRABLES

"They make the hero handsome
to pervert the minds of children."

Ten years old, sassy, and just beginning
to doubt God, when my father took me
to a movie about a poor man who stole
a loaf of bread for his wife and infant.
It was an old film, grainy and blurred
as the boundary between right and wrong.
Later I said I pitied the man, already
a little in love with his pompadour
and animal grace. "Stealing? You approve
of stealing?" my father's look branding me
as criminal. "But they were starving!"
I cried. "That's decadence masquerading
as compassion." He saw through my desire
for a father as handsome, as corruptible.
I persisted, until my father reached out
and struck me twice across the face,
so scrupulous his devotion to the law
he renounced the passion of a young girl.

10

OUR FATHER

God Himself, in all His righteous wrath
could not have been more terrifying
than when you raised your fist and thundered,
"Donnerwetter noch mal!"
Plates trembled, water spilled
and we froze, waiting for
your lightning hand to strike.

That ponderous daughter you admonished,
"Open your mouth, say something!"
now lectures groups of men about computers.
The younger girl you thought would have it
easy, the one you tried to toughen up,
today pays to be heard and weaves words
which do not support her in the style
to which she never grew accustomed.

True, we do owe you our lives: paranoia's
useful in uncertain times. Hearing
distant troops, you forced Mother to flee
Czechoslovakia. How could you know
the shadows of those who died rose
at night to do their lone soft shoe?
And I, how could I know when I played
at your feet, you still heard boots.

HEARING HIM TALK

Eric Heymann, 1903-1957

My own father died of swine flu, spent
his days reading Talmud in the back
room while my mother ran the store,
work-horse daughter of horse thieves.
That was my stock: one foot in heaven,
the other in mud. Never forgot that.

War already brewing when I first danced
with your mother in Karlsbad, she making
eyes at that dark Hungarian who looked
like Robert Taylor, American film star.
I know she didn't think much of me, though
for a stout man I dance a mean tango.

Followed her back to Prague with clear
intentions, ended up yelling at that
chicken-brained idiot who was her best
friend's brother, he believing Hitler
wouldn't invade: too well-off to be smart.
Hand-delivered twelve long-stemmed roses.

Had to drag your mother out. The others
perished. No matter how bad things are
they can always get worse. Stay liquid.
Avoid real estate, handsome men. Choose
one like a rock. Never cheat on taxes.
This country deserves every dime.

Sometimes I have no patience with lumps
in the horseradish sauce, you girls
for refusing to practice your scales.
I go up and down with the market.
You shouldn't take it so hard.
A lot of noise. The way I am.

COMING OF AGE

Dressed and coiffed and openly searching
for eyes of approval, enter my mother,
Loretta Young, sweeping dress into line,
her body attuned to each raised eyebrow,
her charming hauteur from another age.
And me, mouth agape, plucking

the hem of my skirt to cover my knees, plucking
up courage to untie my tongue, searching
for clever words, so clever for my age,
and if not artless, then cuter than mother
so father behind the newspaper would show an eyebrow
or maybe even an eye to me (hardly next in line).

I'd be obvious, mimicking, out of line.
My older sister, fat, lugubrious, plucking
the specks of dust from her lap, furrowed eyebrow
downturned on books, the floor, searching
for ways to escape my coldly beautiful mother
who knew my sister would always be homely; it wasn't
   her age.

And later, when blooming, I came of age
the boys long and gangly stood in line
and gazed enraptured first at my mother
till I came downstairs, plucking
a daisy, hoping, always searching
for proof of affection in an eyebrow.

Does he love me, does he not, for the eyebrow
behind the paper denied me, no matter the age.
No matter he died. I was fourteen, still searching
for the proper gesture, the exact line
to stop the endless critical plucking
at each imperfection. My mother

endured his erratic eruptions. My mother
knew by a flick of her wrist, a raised eyebrow
she could get him to bed, he plucking
clothes from her body, she shedding years from his age.
We never had a chance, there was no line
to help my sister or me. We're still searching.

My mother before the mirror plucking
an eyebrow ruthlessly, searching
for lines of creeping age.

EXCURSION

I

How easily we seem to abandon
our port of origin, bearing ourselves
to a foreign sun. And how the native
fascinates, the way he chooses, say
a melon or a domestic pet. We want
to learn the customs, how to greet
or take leave according to the fashion,
whether to raise an arm for hello, or
for farewell. Finally, we want to own
the way of seeing that underlies
a language, as if we could put on
a new life by slipping into another
mother tongue. Those who never leave
the shore wave white handkerchiefs,
convinced all voyage ends at the crease
of the horizon. And how last week
I could imagine an exotic floral
shirt, crumpled in a heap, discarded,
and how I wanted it, not you, but it,
incessantly, without consolation,
and how I satisfied myself alone
and I was not sad.

II

How last week I wanted
it, not you, but it,
incessantly, without
consolation, and how
I satisfied myself alone
and it was not sad.
How desire's nothing
but the will to own, not
the body, but the mind
it inhabits, or not
the mind but how it talks,
its cadences, the way
of seeing that underlies
a language, and finally,
not the vision but the actual
history, as if we could put on
another life by learning how
it garners information,
the way it chooses, say
a melon or a domestic pet.
Each person greets or takes
leave in a particular fashion —
one raises an arm for hello,
another, farewell. All those cruise ships
in the Caribbean, the Aegean,
how crowded they are with travelers
baring themselves to a foreign
sun, seeking nurture in
another mother tongue.

PROXIMAL DESIRE

I guess I'm talking about the mind. It sleeps around.
— Albert Goldbarth, "Distances"

It's true. Mine sleeps around. Slips
into something sheer. The primordial
body fumbles in dark. Mind craves
its ration of light.

"How you do snuggle up," you say,
as you tempt me with gifts of disclosure.
As though "secret" and "mystery" were one,
and both could be cracked like walnuts.

Muein. Close the lips. The Greek root
of mystery. Something like telling
a guppy not to kiss. I say, "Open!"
and you spill your tragic beans.
I am swollen, replete, trembling
in temporary bliss. How transparent
I am and my hunger for clarity,
a fish swimming out of its bones.

II

THE MIRACLE OF BUBBLES

A woman drives to the video store
to rent a movie. It is Saturday night,
she is thinking of nothing in particular,
perhaps of how later she will pop popcorn
or hold hands with her husband and pretend
they are still in high school. On the way home
a plane drops from the sky, the wing shearing
the roof of her car, killing her instantly.
Here is a death, it could happen to any of us.
Her husband will struggle the rest of his days
to give shape to an event that does not mean
to be understood. Since memory cannot operate
without plot, he chooses the romantic — how young
she was, her lovely waist, or the ironic — if only
she had lost her keys, stopped for pizza.

At the precise moment the plane spiraled
out of control, he was lathering shampoo
into his daughter's hair, blonde and fine
as cornsilk, in love with his life, his
daughter, the earth (for "cornsilk" is how
he thought of her hair), in love with the miracle
of bubbles, how they rise in a slow dance,
swell and shimmer in the steamy air, then
dissolve as though they never were.

LEST THE BRIGHTNESS ANNIHILATE

Today I woke longing for
the silk rug I didn't buy
for the hallway. Persian Art
was going out of business
and offered me a good deal.
"If you want to throw away money,"
you said, "give it to me."

How dull we are in our separate
convictions, pulling away from
each other like workaday beasts.
Even the pebbles under our feet
settle back to a more intimate
proximity. You want me the way

a medieval monk wants solitude,
prays to make himself whole.
I want to walk in a handknotted field
of blues and ivories. If I stray
near the tree of punishment, dyed
red with madder and sheep's blood,

angels intercede, and Allah himself,
face hidden by twenty thousand veils.
Beyond borders that bind and unify
lies the manifold universe, you and I
clothing ourselves in threadbare desire
lest the brightness annihilate.

THE SUCCULENT EDGE

Everybody wants them in the woods, but nobody
wants them in the garden.
          — John Mitchell, "White-tail Deer"

It is open season for stags
only. Hunters refuse to kill
antlerless deer, turning
this Connecticut hill town
into a whitetail kitchen:
stubs for fir, skeletons
for hemlock. A doe in rut
once trampled a woman
without provocation.

I have written a friend in Alaska,
Send wolves. I have written a friend
in Tanzania, *Send lion's blood.*
I have even collected the clippings
from barbershops, stuffed them
into the toes of discarded pantyhose
and strung them along the trees
bordering my property. It was breached
that same night.

Now with a bound, one clears the wire
barrier between woodland and garden,
devouring begonias in search of sumac
and sassafras. So merciless
in her hunger, I suddenly think, Sister,
are we so very different, craving
as we do, surfeit for the belly,
buckskin for the back.

I KNOW WHY I AM HERE

I made one small hole in the breast
pocket of my husband's hunting jacket.
He loves this jacket, faded dull green
from early morning rain. I have done
my work neatly with his pocket-knife.
He will not be able to trace the incision
back to me. I have committed this act
because his arms are too short, his kisses
too dry and because he double-checks
doorknobs before departures.

I know why I am here, in the brass bed
of my lover. It is partly hunger, partly
love. I have brought strawberries
for the occasion. He buries them
one by one between my thighs, then sucks
them out whole, saying they taste of musk,
having ripened in darkness.

One day my husband will discover the damaged
pocket, and will ache with the loss of perfect
fabric. It is vital to add he is allergic
to dust and berries of all kinds, and thus
cannot partake of my legitimate fruit.

NIGHT WATCH

Give desire a shape, no matter
if that shape be squalor or sailor,
bronzed, blue-eyed, with muscles
of a man addicted to lifting weights.
You ache to touch his forearms.

Give him moves, subtle, deliberate,
and foreknowledge of where to put
his plate. Make it night. Have him
strip, swim the length of the turquoise
pool. Don't jump in. Listen instead

to the voluptuous rhythm of his wake.
When he emerges, naked, the water
dripping from his skin, it is you
who are exposed. Are you happier
for it, to know you could not bear

the tension of a slow seduction?
You choose this drama to unfold
as monologue, the way you will
replay this scene, your fierce
longing, and how you were taken.

LATE NIGHT REPORT

Murder, assassination, a plane crash,
late Sunday night and the bad news
rolls in like a sermon. We sit,
stuffed and lazy from too much
food, football, imperfect love.
This morality play by the network
must be designed to pull us back
to the daily, as if we had grown soft
from our small dose of pleasure.
That sudden slap on a newborn's rump,
surely there's a better way. The message
is clear — you've had it easy so far kid,
welcome to the world. Now the news

and the vivid shots of all our possible
violent fates if we don't repent, and
we don't. "I'd think," you say, voice
tinged with sarcasm, "you'd like this cup
of tea, since you relish the dark side."
He's referring to my refusal this morning.
"It's one thing in the abstract," I reply,
"quite another to have your nose rubbed
in it." I'm referring to his appetite
for excess. The next story comes on
and it is a fire. We both burst out
laughing, a cry of a sort.

THE GIFT

I

For his fortieth birthday a woman decides
to offer her husband a gift: he can tie her up
and have his way with her. If he gags her
with the terrycloth belt from his bathrobe,
she will be unable to protest. She goes
to the hardware store to buy rope, the kind
used to prevent boats from slipping away
from their moorings. All day she imagines
what her amenable husband will do — spank
her perhaps, but only playfully. What if
the game takes a more serious turn, if he
exults in his new-found power, beats her till
she's senseless or tickles her with a feather?
She consults with a friend over the phone.
Do it, the friend advises, he will be
your slave forever. The woman considers:
she has her eye on a new Persian carpet.
He could take her on it, his eyes rolling
with lust in their sockets. He'll pinch
her breasts, leave toothmarks on the exposed
skin of her neck. She will writhe her head
from side to side, try to call out "uncle"
through the thick wad of cloth stuffed in
her mouth. Imagining this she recalls her father
who spanked her bare rump when she was defiant,
and how pure she felt then, how justified.

II

A man comes home after a tedious day
at the office. His wife greets him
in a pink robe with babydoll sleeves.
"Happy birthday," she says, handing him
a hank of rope. "Tie me up and have
your way with me." The man's spirits
revive, though he's peeved she has not
first prepared dinner. But he's a good
sport and busies himself at her ankles.
Hard work this, he thinks, he's forgotten
everything he learned in the Boy Scouts.
Tying her wrists to the bedposts presents
more of a challenge. Soon he's grumbling:
he slaves all day, comes home to yet more
demands. After she is securely fastened,
he stands back to survey his handiwork.
He notes the mole on her ear, the muscular
thighs, the thin line of hair at her navel.
Then the phone rings and it is the hospital
saying his mother is in a coma. He dresses
hastily, grabs his car keys, departs. Hours
later he returns to his wife tangled up
in the bedroom. "The story of our lives,"
she snarls. "Your mother has always come first."
He heads for the kitchen, pops a chicken
pot pie in the microwave, most pleased and
astonished the knots he has tied still hold.

THE WORLD'S MOST FABULOUS LOVER

A woman enters the bedchamber
of the world's most fabulous lover.
No candles, no tray laden with grapes,
no raw oysters. He's watching T.V.
in his undershirt. He's swilling beer
from a can. When he belches he doesn't
cover his mouth. How hairy he is, fibrisae
sprouting from nostrils and earlobes.
She sits on a stool at his feet.
After waiting so long, what's a few
minutes more? The referee makes
a bad call and the man shakes a fist,
grabs the remote, says, "You might
as well take off your clothes."
The woman complies. She has nothing
to lose. Now the news announces
the collision between an oil truck
and a busload of children. "Tell me,"
the man says, pulling her onto his lap,
"of your former lovers." This is foreplay?
She shrugs, tells about the man who came
with his eyes open, about doing it
in the closet of the Waldorf Astoria
with the maid unlatching the door,
of the man who kept up a steady stream
of chatter. "What did he say?" he asks.
"Baby baby baby," she replies. "Baby baby baby,"
he says. Now she's surprised. Her body's
performing with amazing agility. Next
she's heaving and panting like a woman
in labor, and then she bears down
and cries out her own name.

VISITATION

"Out in the moon too long,"
they say, and stroke
her cheek reflectively.
Even as they nod,
her eyebrows are turning white.

Mercury hovers just above
freezing. Elsewhere, tides rise
and fall out of season.
She rocks, content,
and knits a coverlet.

One night she hears a
creaking sound, the moon
walking the floor.
As she leans forward,
it rolls from her tongue.

ALBANIAN VIRGIN

If a girl of the Klementi tribe fiercely objected
to the proposed marriage, a blood feud could only
be avoided by her swearing an oath that she would
never marry. Such a woman was called an Albanian
Virgin and ranked in the tribe as a man.
— Carolyn Heilbrun, *Reinventing Womanhood*

1

The way he caught that horsefly
midair, the way he grinds his heel
into the dirt, taking pleasure
in the spider's slow death, the way
he throws a look at me as though
he already owns me —
I do not consent.

I shall smoke with the men.
I have seen them in the greying
light, their weapons close
to them always.

2

The day is hot. My hair
is cropped. It is so still
I hear the bells clank
from the field. I swear the oath
before twelve witnesses
to forsake the intimate gestures
of all men, to remain chaste
as an unfreshened goat.

This night spent in solitude
on a rush mat, alone with the gravity
of my own body.

3

I have learned to clip
the horns of goats, to slit
the throats of sheep
so the warm blood bathes
my fingers, and the animal feels
no pain, so sharp is my blade.

I am carried by dreams to the field
where I lie on the earth flanked by goats,
push a pale wet form from my loins.
It struggles to rise on its spindly legs.
I look deep into my goat-child's eyes.

4

I eat with the men.
I chew charred slabs of meat
with the men. We smoke together,
my rough trousers chafing
the flesh of my thighs.

I gaze at the women who sit
in tight circles, pounding
pestles into stone bowls.

My lungs fill
with harsh comforting smoke.

HONEYMOON

The climate here is hot and dry.
It is the slack season, a time
of alternate bearing. Olive groves
in full blossom will not be harvested
until October, when we shall be gone
from this place where women snake
through narrow streets, backs
hunched over their losses.

In the taverna you swill ouzo like a sailor
spinning yarns of defloration. You rise
to join the weaving line of dancing men
and smash glass with the rest of them.

Outside, a bone-white chip of moon,
and the sea spread out like a black
tablecloth. I want it back, I want
it back, silk web of flesh, crescent
membrane, I want it back. I finger
my amber worry beads, there is no
bead missing.

Today for lunch there was fish with wide
open eyes. We were told to eat the gelatinous
mass, it would give us second sight. The fish
lay on a bed of overripe tomatoes, seeds
spilling off the fork.

Our coupling has been quick and hard and secret.
You, fish, have bitten my wormlike lips.
With eyes sealed shut, thinlipped mouth gulping

for water, you struggle, caught in a net.
Your toes twitch as you fall off the rim
of the world into the black dish of sleep.
Your eyes dart under the folds of your lids,
like minnows in freshwater.

O stickleback, humpback, black dromedary,
pitted olive, we hoard our losses.
Today when I stooped to pick up your socks,
my backbone locked and I couldn't stand up.

UNINVITED GUESTS

Three can keep a secret if two are corpses.
— Yiddish folk saying

Even the dead can't keep
a secret. They barge in,
sit at your table, demanding
to be served. They bang
their spoons like children
crying, *Feed me! Feed me!*
and you have never prepared
enough.
      Once you would have welcomed
the dead, begged Mother to set out
extra plates. But now they consume
what was promised to the living.
They climb into the marriage bed
with their own unearthly linen,
whispering old secrets you wish
they would keep to themselves.

THIS TERRIBLE THING CALLED LOVE

It's not what you thought, that constant
leap, ardor of blood, tumult of union,
the oh oh oh in the dark

nor priced as you thought, the caught
breath at a moment of some inattention.
You put on an insouciant smile.

You've been together for years now, an old
married couple, yet last night you fled
from home in bedroom slippers and white
bunny jacket. It was late. It was cold.
You wanted to run from this terrible thing,
call it rage, call it love. The car
wouldn't start.

When it did, you parked outside a neighbor's
house. You thought you'd freeze in your baby-
blue station wagon. It got later. You ran
out of cigarettes. You imaged the morning
headline: *Matron Succumbs to Hypothermia
Half Block from Home.*

The motor jumped as you started the car,
made the U turn, pulled into your own
driveway. The lights were on, illuminating
the stained glass window. You hoped he was filled
with remorse. The knob wouldn't budge.
He had bolted the door from the inside.

The sound of the bell was a cry of surrender.
He opened at once, but you stomped up the stairs
like a big girl. How not to think of this man
as the enemy, how to break through this unholy
deadlock, this terrible thing called love?

AND SHE IS STILL ALIVE

When I took your hand and consented
to go out into the wide world, how
could I know the spindleshanked crone
followed? I swept the floors tidy
and clean, attempted to keep her
at bay. For years in the forest
of sleep, I thrashed my way through
the underbrush, came face to face
with the same creature and was struck
dumb. Starlings flew in my hair,
disrupting everything. Last night
we spat out those ugly words, refused
to own them, give them names. I thought
we were safe in our gingerbread house
but the red-hot oven beckoned
and we hurled ourselves in.

WHAT I DWELL ON

We never come to thoughts. They come to us.
— Martin Heidegger

It has been months since a good
night's sleep, that landing you come
to at the foot of the stairs. Instead,
two-hour catnaps before springing
awake as though what is required of me
is vigilance. I cannot tell you
what I think walking the long corridor
to the kitchen for a sip of juice, or
wandering into my son's room to examine
his face, the radical purity of something
not quite formed. At night the face becomes
more like itself, bones make their minor
shifts and settle, like a house sinking
as it contracts, the pliant earth
rising up to receive it, even the windows,
the vanishing roof. When a man jumps
from a great height he dies of suffocation,
not impact. I fear those twin perils, and
falling, now falling asleep. Miser or thief,
I hold to what I know. No one sneaks up
from behind, pushes me over the balustrade.
And no one would claim me, breathless
and shattered from the depths of sleep.

III

NÉE MAGGIE MALONE

She didn't shave her legs or underarms
because her husband said it was unnatural
which is fine in Zagreb but in summer
heat at the Safeway she felt savage
like when she'd had to go in the middle of
the night at his family's farmhouse and relieved
herself in a pot which she hid in the closet.

That summer the pick-up died while he was restoring
houses on Capitol Hill for "that bastard Grodski
doesn't he know I'm craftsman   no bubbles when I
paint walls" and that summer Rudy still suckled at
Maggie's breast though he was four and her female
friends thought it bizarre even perverse.

What would they say if they knew he crawled nightly
into their bed wetting the sheets   Maggie
stumbling for the child's cot while father and son
slept on together.

Then he was fired by that bastard Grodski who said
he was arrogant and Maggie told friends he quit
because he couldn't take orders from a crook
who didn't appreciate fine work.

They were poorer next summer and he said "Save money
make sheets" and she thought about it   then he said
"Be useful   learn Croatian" and he gave her a dictionary
and she tried in late afternoons to say the sounds

while the new baby nursed and Rudy clung monkey-like
to her furry legs.

Irish jigs played on the phonograph   she thought
I should make sheets   I should learn Croatian
she hummed the reels thinking   I'd like to
shuffle stomp stomp stomp shuffle stomp stomp stomp

MADAME KARENINA IN THE GARDEN

Vengeance is mine, and I will repay.

The garden columbine and marigold
unfold their petals to a blazing sun.
Behind me, Alexei speaks in monotone,
his knuckles crack, punctuate the drone.
I count my heartbeats one by one.

A watering can sits on the pedestal.
I reach out for it, and it falls.
Alexei stoops to set it right,
reiterates the law of God and Man.
A pool of water seeps into the ground.

Each uttered syllable, relentless, rhythmic,
like a train, takes me back to Moscow,
mazurkas, a black satin ribbon encircling
my throat, a brooch of three drooping pearls.
We dance, the other Alexei and I.

His teeth gleam, the dove-grey fabric
of his uniform crushed against my cheek,
the scent of musk between us, persistent
as breath. Someone is drowning.
A momentary silence pulls me back.

I arrange my curls, my smile, a quick retort:
"Such a fuss," I say. "A simple tête à tête
about diet, the benefits of oats or hay,
when to give the crop, and when to let
the horse run free." Shocking, how easily

I imitate the casual shrug, the exact lilt
of unconcern. How naturally it comes, deceit.
The trick is not to look him in the eye.
Then all things are possible — a request
for extra rubles: the seamstress must be paid.

My gowns have all been altered, taken in.
I've lost my appetite for food, for sweets,
since I am famished for one thing only
and that requires abandoning restraint.
Something is broken. My body slims.

Sometimes I think I am but mare myself,
gallop stored in fetlock, hoof, glistening
coat. Those sounds I make, grunt and moan,
when I am ridden hard, when I buckle under,
bestial in my blind devouring love.

A QUESTION OF AESTHETICS

He never wrote a letter without
the words "despair" or "terror"
as in, "Even as a child I knew
despair," or, "How to turn
this terror into art." How romantic
it seemed then, like living
a Russian novel. His final note
read, "Tell her our relationship
was fully satisfying in every way."

No one ever says how thrilling
pain is, how it takes you like
a lover, how your body cringes
before surrender. At first
you cry no, no, then swoon
into its burly arms. You should see
your open mouth, your breath coming
in harsh gasps. Trust pain to find
the choicest part, the marrow,
and suck out resolve, leaving you
limp. But oh, how you'll sleep.

The only burden heavier than pain
is boredom, want of danger. When I
teach *Anna Karenina* to young girls,
I say, "Every woman should experience
one disastrous love affair and survive."
How like a woman Anna was, to hesitate
because she could not bear to throw
her red purse away. How like a man

he was to put a bullet some place deadly.
As a woman who's survived, I see boredom
now as comfort, devotion as something
precious, and death in any form,
a slap across the face.

SONG WHILE ARRANGING JASMINE AND JEWELWEED

1

You ask me, when did it begin?
When I saw you at the mercado
sniffing a cantaloupe. Ramon!
The way you held that melon it must
have ripened in your hand. That night
in the ballroom, it was your sparkling
moustache, the pearl stud in your tie.
And when you entered me it was as though
you already knew me, so sure was your beat,
so emphatic my reply. Adorado! I told you
I had many lovers. You knew I lied.

2

When you give me that cock-
eyed, cross-eyed, pie-eyed
look, oh my pet I know
you're feeling the itch
to travel. That's when
I stick a rose in my hair,
light a cigarillo and offer
to button your spanking white
shirt. Adios, Ramon, bye bye!
I shut the door with finesse
and greet my own heart, sweet
heart, faithful dumb pumper.

3

Take care where you plant your feet,
my Latin-American strongman.
There's a hot tarantella on the tip
of my tongue. Don't tell me to shut
my mouth. I say what I please.
And if there's an earthquake, I get
the doorway. So there's a dead one
floating in the milk. A cockroach here
can be rocked in a cradle. I don't
wear these pointy shoes for nothing.
I am no dumb blonde you swept away.
I play my part with proper agitation.

4

It's Sunday, and here comes Ramon.
All is forgiven, my docile lambkin!
Let's bleat together under the covers.
Come nuzzle the pale globe of my belly,
come drink from my goblet of love.

PRODIGAL

To the rear of the grocery store in Bethlehem,
New Hampshire, nomad compound bows are mounted
on pegboards, sold to locals who prefer to hunt
deer "the hard way." Each summer Hasidim

swarm to this town, stay in hotels like the Arcadia
which advertises GOLF in Hebrew. They come here
for the rarified mountain air, for each other,
and because they have always come here. Main Street

swells with men in shiny black suits, who nod
in passing and twirl their damp earlocks.
Their women lounge in aluminum chairs, sweat in wigs
and shapeless cotton prints. They tug their white

anklets, complain about the price of cleanser.
The recent scandal concerns one Mordecai Katz,
kosher butcher from the Bronx, who, in his recent
bereavement, cupped his palms around a cashier's

ample rump, cried out, "My little shiksa, tender
brisket!" Jewel (for that was her name), slapped
his hands like a horse tail swats flies. In the end
no charges were filed against Mordecai, in deference

to his age and general condition. The Hasidim swore to keep an eye on him, but old Mordecai slipped out at night, for morning found remnants of soft-shelled crab on his rumpled trousers.

A match was attempted with Rosalie, the spinster seamstress, who was not altogether unwilling, but the feckless Mordecai had already developed a taste for treyf, a taste for meat on the cloven hoof.

SUBTITLES

There was always something forbidden
about foreign films, as though reading
subtitles afforded a glimpse into
the still untranslated adult world.
I had to board a bus, then walk up

Lefferts Boulevard, past outdoor fish
stalls and enormous-breasted women
guarding fruit. In this flourishing
neighborhood was *The Circle,* the one
theatre in Queens that featured

foreign films. It was here I saw
Kurasawa's *Yojimbo,* warrior gone amuck
with exquisite swordplay. A human wrist
carried off by a dog while the town
smolders, the wreckage so complete

nothing is left whole. This is the end
result of formal perfection — Samurai
turned mercenary; an old man trussed-up,
suspended from a tree, knowing he's safer
where he is. So when the man next to me

places his hand on my thigh, I sit in my
plush seat and say nothing. On screen
the hero drinks hot blood. Already he
is outdated. And in the dark, a touch
light and tentative, perhaps imagined.

CLOSE CALL

Last night you appeared in a dream
wearing my grandfather's coat,
the one I search for in thrift shops,
still angry my mother gave it away.

Last night the faded herringbone
hung on you like an old sack,
that breadline look to your face.

You were trying to steal my food.
I had to turn you in. Consider yourself
reported for attempted theft.

You turned your back and shuffled
away. I ran to wrap my arms
around your spare form, my breasts
pressing the cloth like
two unpeeled potatoes.

It is I, it is I who accuse you
of exposing my terrible hunger
which would fill even the pockets
of Grandfather's voluminous coat.

HOW THE PAST INHABITS

When she was twelve, my mother
contracted scarlet fever, before
antibiotics, before the war
would make living in Bohemia
obsolete. Now she is twelve,
she wants to sing in the opera,
paint her lips red, wear gowns
that expose her shoulders.

Soon she will walk in the orchard
with her brother, the one she lifted
aloft with a fireplace poker while
he slept, an infant swaddled in linen
in his bassinet. Now it is spring
and the tiny hard green apples
fit neatly in her palms. They smell
tart and spicy, as yet unripened

by a blowzy summer sun. She is about
to take a bite, though the apples
are unripe and she is only recently
completely well. Her lips hover
over the unblemished skin. Suddenly
her father, following secretly behind,
strikes them from her hand.
This is how much he loves her

though the line between protection
and possession is unclear. Is this
the story I want to tell? Or how
later she begs him to flee to America
and he refuses, saying, What would I do,
an old man of sixty, sell sausages
in a foreign land? He and his wife
will die prematurely and his son,

the boy who walks in the orchard,
will survive because he knows how
to weld. And my mother will take
sleeping pills night after night
to prevent her father from surfacing
even in dream. Her granddaughters
sing beautifully, but my mother
frets daily over what she should eat.

NIGHT AT THE OPERA

Although Aida and Rhadames are buried alive
in a crypt, they sing a long and complicated
duet which requires much breath. I want
to cry out, "Save air!" because I am eight
and living long is of great concern to me
and I don't understand that kind of love.
Only synagogue bores me more than opera
and for a similar reason: nothing makes sense.
During the High Holy Days, guttural sounds
engulf me, and there is all this standing up
and sitting down. The congregants seem
more intrigued by each other than by God.
One commandment says not to covet. I don't
know what that means, but I love the word.
It reminds me of my favorite blanket, its
much-nuzzled satin binding. I've been told
to give it up, but I can't, nor my thumb, most
faithful companion. My feet throb, cramped
in black Maryjanes. On stage, the lovers
swoon into each other's arms and die, while
overhead, hymns and sacred dance continue
without my participation or consent.

WHAT WE SHALL BECOME

From these heights the war
blazes in primary colors, banners
magnificent. From here the scale

of human suffering is inconsequential.
Down there, under the hooves, clumps
of dirt churn and fly, bodies fall.

What alters if the gods pity or mock us?
Once there was a great Lord who sired
three sons — one foolish, one bloodthirsty,

one noble and true. They turn on each other
like wild dogs. When reconciliation seems
almost possible, a musket misfires, picks off

the noble son. He drops to the ground,
stone dead. His father learns the meaning
of *random universe,* clutches his throat

and chokes. This story repeats itself
generation after generation. Our hearts
will always go out to a man at the brink

of lunacy, since we seem to fear losing
our wits even more than our lives. Is there
salt in the castle strongroom? There is

always salt. Salt for the preservation
of meat, a rival's severed head, to remind us
of what we once were, what we have replaced.

ERENDIRA REMEMBERS

My grandmother took my palm,
smooth and blank as a dolphin's
back. She predicted
I would make a journey soon
over water. I had begun

to disbelieve in water.
We had been rooted
to these barrens for as long
as I remembered. The wind

filled my nostrils with a dust
so thick I could not smell
the sea, or salt.
My grandmother brought me men
who crossed miles of desert
to enter my tent. I wrapped

my legs around their waists
and whispered, Tell me
of your travels. I never
travel, but even swerved
at the moment of birth
to evade the midwife's grasp.

Then a fairheaded boy
gave me a bracelet
of hammered gold and aquamarine.
He spoke of fish that glowed
phosphorescent. I licked

the sweat from his bronzed back
and was happy. I knew

he would kill for me.
I gave him the knife.
Blood poured from the old woman's mouth
in a torrent. Then the rains came
and washed away everything.
Lines appeared on my palm.

IV

FIRST THERE WAS LIGHT AND THAT
BEGINS THE NARRATIVE

1. *Genealogy*

Then there was hunger, then
there was blame. Even God must
be ambivalent about knowing.

We know what happens to travelers
their first day out — shame,
exaltation. Fingerthick dust

on trees invites them to leave
a mark. When Adam knew Eve
she bore him Cain, *kaniti,*

I acquired. Adam, for the moment
so besotted by birth, he forgives
everything. Next Abel, wet-breath,

not lasting. Who can fault Eve
for preferring him? How sweet
to adore the one who most wholly

responds. The boys spend childhood
bickering, Cain, grim, tenacious,
burdened by the weight of expectation,

and Abel, lighthearted and wily.
He has no need to hoard. When God
reenters the story, Cain will rise up

against his brother, quarrel over
God's affection, poor substitute
for mother love. First

there was light and that began
the narrative. All events,
a fulfillment. Even mistakes.

2. *Earthly Fare*

Lizard, foxglove, piglet, Adam
busies himself in the Garden
naming, syllables spilling
out of his mouth so that even
while steeped in contemplation,
wildebeest, redbud, he cannot stop.
He babbles, delights in the pitch
of his voice, until exhausted
he falls into slumber, awakens
to Woman, fully formed. God knows
he needs conversation, but she's
had no childhood to speak of
and hers is a world already
defined. Under munificent leaves
of the fig tree and under the vast
dome of sky, Adam's stuttering fingers
explore her. She's asking questions
like who and wherefore and why and just
because He says so? and reaches out
for what pleases her eye. It tastes
good and she doesn't die. Her baby
Abel, wet-breath, not lasting, he
shows her how. No one prepared
her, no mother with sweetcakes
who crooned lullabies, no mother at all,
just no and you can't, without
explanation. So like a father not
to embellish, no margin for error, no
one more chance. He had no mother either,
no honey with the bitter pill, no push
and pull, only a stunning shock of light.

3. *After Eden*

If she had known the gestures
of reproach, dark scowls, the stony
back, lingered, she'd have prayed
harder for a little girl, named her
something silly and inconsequential,
like Fleur or Belle, not burdened her
with the task of making it right
between them. But as it was, Cain,
acquisition, was meant to buy back
Adam's love. So there were strings.
Small wonder he grew sharp-featured
as a rodent, sniffed the air to test
if it was safe to breathe. She couldn't
bear the look of him. And close
as breath was memory of drought,
the year thistle and sting-bush
flourished, and sustenance, a thin
gruel of tuber and barley. Eve,
heavy again with child, turned
inward, left Cain to wander after
his father in the pock-marked clay.
Then Eve, flanked by starving cows,
crouched in the parched field and then
the wet slippery child sliding out,
strands of fine black hair tracing
its skull, and the cows rearranging
their loosened flesh as Eve held
the child to her breast. "Wet-breath,"
she called him, because his birth
augured rain. And when it came,
the earth unfolded, a paradise of green.

4. *Gift of the Firstborn*

Cain should have known when he prepared
a platter of pomegranate, fig and plum,
she'd turn around and give it to his brother,
sick again with croup. She babied him, let
his hair grow long and woolly as fleece.
His father was no better, obsessed with crop
rotation. Only in dreams was he extravagant
with signs of love. Because there'd been no
hail that year, and the rains, plentiful,
Cain filled a sack with leftover fruit,
offered it to God. He too showed no regard,
spoke of "crouching demons" devouring
Cain's heart. Yet Abel's gift, the firstborn
of his flock, smoke singeing its fatty parts,
pleased Him. It was too much, too much
for any man to bear. Cain cursed
his brother with every ugly word he knew,
tore his face, his thick resilient hair,
then grabbed a stick and beat him dead.
Rhubarb blades. Blackthorn. The pungent
odor of mint. His senses never felt more keen.
No word yet for what he'd done. The firmament
ignited, a multitude of nameless stars.

5. *Granted One*

At first she thought God loved
her most, to have dealt her such
affliction. It proved she was
His special girl. Not that Adam
didn't care, just more accustomed
to the vagaries of weather, wind
and rain and never the same day
twice. Then too, he was so grateful
Cain survived, he became almost tender,
too late to halt Eve's descent
into an absence of recall. She wandered
the fields, stripping the husks off
sheaves of corn, and making dolls
for "little Fleur." She whispered
incessantly to her and sang strange
rhyming songs. When Adam tried
to bring her back, she accused him
of intruding. The dolls crowded
their bed at night and sat with them
at supper. And thus time passed.
Eve's hair turned brittle, then grey,
so that once when she caught sight
of herself, she greeted that woman
with polite reserve. One spring, mist
shrouding the meadows like baby's breath,
Adam came to her with all the need
and urgency of a young man. The tilt
of his head, his shyly offered bouquet
of blossoms, reminded her of Abel
and Eve lay down and took him in.
Afterwards, she wept. Another son
was born, Shet, *Granted One.*

V

A FORMER PHILOSOPHY STUDENT
ADDRESSES ISSUES RAISED
BY HER PROFESSOR

— *for George Tovey*

EPISTEMOLOGY

How do we know what we know?
This much is sure: surpass
the seductiveness of the visible.
Honeysuckle, hollyhock, the glistening
moisture on a purple grape, all
delight the senses, but leap to the next
order of being, that ideal state where
things dwell in their thingness in Platonic
harmony, or delve into the dark epicenter
of chaotic disarray. The nature of experience,
that issue of reality, is something.
Maybe not. I don't know.

METAPHYSICS

And what is the nature of ultimate
reality? I mean, the underpinning
of everything. Is is singular,
stark, austere, or polygamous,
flamboyant as a hot flamenco,
dance of Siva? Possibilities
are endless. Each has its draw.
Consider it all.

ETHICS

What is the right and just course
of action? Not the expedient, this
we knew when we were smart enough
to spell handkerchief. An examined
life goes beyond the pleasure principle,
the transitory smack of flesh. We are
born hedonists, don't we know it, but
upon reaching the age of consent
we must consent to consider what is
categorical. And what imperative.
For goodness sake.

AESTHETICS

The bastard branch. Denied
its legal share, and yet
the soul of the matter.
Whether a thing is beautiful
and whether absolutely.
This poem, for instance:
do the lines break at the perfect
place, does the image of the grape
resonate, reveal a truth beyond
metaphor? These issues with which
I wrestle are my stock in trade:
profound respect for shade of meaning,
desire to unearth the roots of words,
logos, love of language. I cannot love
without abuse, from time to time crack-
ing apart the syllables, reaching for
the milky white pearl inside, then
wringing the sense out.

AND THEN

And then there is the man himself,
beyond prototype, beyond ideal, but
human and emphatically particular:
the way his hair when ruffled
by the wind defied the law
of gravity, the way he loped
with long-legged grace across
the centuries, seeking sustenance
from the mind itself, wondering.
Soft-spoken, patient, the opposite
of charismatic, this charioteer
gripped the reins with a serene
touch. We trusted him, followed
at our own speed. Above all,
recognizing the immateriality of destination,
but learning a way of travel.

BALANCING ACT

Up here on the high wire it's a sheer
sure-footed dance, a one-night mission
under the Big Top, without a safety net

to cushion. It's the taunting misstep,
the sharp intake of breath, exhalations
of the squeamish egging me on, and the world

marble-smooth, veined to the core, perched
on the tip of my tongue. I juggle spangled
orbs from one palm to another, a marriage

of holding on and letting go. You'd think
by now I'd let it fall, the world cracked
open like a skull, bits of hair, feathers,

the loose associations. But once I knew
the buttons on a fly, the upturned collar,
the child licking her fingers imagining

an Africa, I knew all matter while compressed
is no longer solitary. Ask me how I keep it
twirling, defying gravity with every turn —

I'll never tell. You won't read fear
in eyes that glitter, dazzle, take you
by storm. Come one, come all, observe

communion with infinity. See the fabulous
steps, the foolhardy toes. Be amazed
by the pupil of possibility.

DEFINITIVE ACT

A magician saws a woman in half
by accident, says, "I guess I need

more practice." He climbs inside
his coffer of mirrors to perfect

his craft. Any fracture increases
the chance for dialogue: "Lady,"

he says, "Illusion makes the body
radiant, makes it bleed." Reader,

you are the errant half I am
longing for, longing to cleave.

★

What a mess she's left, the lamp
still burning, scattered hairpins,
her spare tutu. She'd insisted

on small amenities, this lamp
for example, its tiffany shade.
Light wasn't the issue, she wanted

things pretty, an intimacy beyond
performance, beyond applause.
She wanted post mortems, to wear

his tuxedo, his top hat, to ruffle
his doves. He wanted to shut her
up, confine her to quarters. Then

down on his knees, like a beggar,
a dog, down on all fours, tongue
at the keyhole, tongue like a key.

★

This isn't a fable, here
is the coffer, the keyhole,
the mirror that saves you
from torpor, from me.

WHEN I LEARN MY FRIEND MUST LOSE
HER BREAST TO CANCER

Remember the old fairytale?
A pea is placed under twenty
mattresses and twenty-eight
eiderdown quilts (the numbers
are quite exact). Perched
high on this nest of feathers
lies a real princess. She tosses
and turns all night. The moral
is not that pampered girls
cannot abide the coarser stuff
of life. No, the princess feels
the hard, round, immovable pea,
feels it intimately, knows its
dimensions. She senses what doesn't
belong, the imperfection bruising
her milky-white skin. Look you,
this is a true story.

★

When you draw the shape of the mass
they removed last week, I see a rat
with a tail, you see a sperm
swimming in your breast. You say,
"If this tumor has a name, its name
is Frank."

Darwin's mother told him when he was so young
he barely remembered, that if he looked deep

enough into a flower's center, that flower
would reveal its name.

Perhaps if I named my breasts, like I named
my children, I would care for them more,
be their proud mother.

★

At the Breast Screening Clinic
I meet Daphne, pink silicone model
with three implanted malignancies.
She teaches me what to search for
when I self-examine.

The mammogram reveals the aquamarine
subterranean world of breasts, an interlacing
network of rivers and streams. An outlaw
could find shelter here for weeks, even years.
Only the keenest arrow could flush him out.
Calcified deposits. Pebble in a granite bed.
Needle in a haystack. Anything suspicious.

But there is a startling beauty here,
a sheer blue expanse with darker
etched tracings. I think of coral
reefs seen through a blue filter.
And the sky blue ribs, like nothing
natural in their perfection: carved
blue ivory tusks. Whatever I am

looking at, it is foreign, pristine,
nothing that I care to touch.

The thermogram measures heat, explodes
in primary colors the breast we've sucked
as infants, violent in its reds
and greens. This is the breast of salt,
of blood, the one we could devour,
the one that could feed us.

★

I want to take away your guilt,
your belief that you are being
punished. "If I survive," you say,
"I will change my life." When I
was seven, I lost my bankbook,
prayed fervently to a benign
God leaning on His elbow,
taking a rest from thunder and other
people's prayers. "If you help me,"
I vowed, "I'll be a good girl forever
and ever." Even then I doubted my word.

I want to give you my white
satin nightshirt, the one
you love so much, with eyelet
at the throat and cuffs.

But you refuse. "I won't
be able to lift my arm."

★

At night I dream of my dead dog.
She wags her tail and drags a charred
useless limb. I try to hack it off,
filled with disgust at the gangrenous
smell. I'm afraid I will catch it.
I believe this in spite of myself.

★

"And how did you sleep last night?"
the princess was asked. "Oh quite
miserably! Goodness knows
what was in my bed. I am black
and blue all over." Then the prince
took her for his wife, and the pea
was placed in a real museum
where it is to this day
unless somebody has carried it off.

★

PATH REPORT: ALL CLEAR

The word when it comes brings reprieve,
not a sentence. The head lifts up
off the chopping block, the neck

slips out from the noose, and a door
clanks shut on a world where a murder
of crows, a bright red mailbox, even
the cold grey sky, is miraculous.
"I will change my life," she'd said,
and the doctors came with their fancy
tools and cut the cancer away. Now
you see it, now you don't. Euphoria
lasted two days.

★

Dinnertime. Family scene. Two daughters,
a husband, a wife. The wife ladles soup
from a green tureen, one breast bobbing
in silicone splendor, the other drooping
its forty-two years. The daughters
squabble with sticks and stones, ignore
their mother's admonitions.

Enraged, suddenly, over what has spilt,
she pours a half-full glass of milk
down her elder daughter's budding chest.
Stricken, the girl flees to her room,
erects a barricade of chairs.
Her mother comes to blow it down.
And the house is made of wood.

THE DESIRE TO BE CONTAINED

In the recurrent dream a low-flying
plane is strafing the countryside.
Bullets spray the ground in a pattern
of hit or miss. I have done nothing
to deserve this. I am digging a tunnel,
bare hands clawing the rocky soil.
If I wedge myself in, the sharpshooter
high in his restless plane will not
see me. I take up so little space.

This is the secret appeal of corners.
And why we love the roof, which we see
as the lid of a pot. The teeming life
inside a house seems wild and uncontained.
And this is why we love mummies, swaddled
in white linen bandages. For isn't
dissolution what we fear most?

I can barely look at astronauts who walk
in space, connected to the mother ship
by a fragile cord. If it were severed,
their lumbering silvery shapes would drift
into deepest blackest space, like stunned
polar bears floating away in utter silence
from all that is remotely known.

ELEMENTAL COSMOLOGY

The rooster crows with his eyes shut
because he crows from memory.
　　　　— Yiddish folk saying

A rooster once crowed with his eyes
open because he wanted to see
the morning unfold. So smitten
was he by the first tinge
of dawn, he stopped singing.
Then the sun ceased her ascent,
feet froze on their way
out of bed, mouths stiffened
into yawns. What will release

this landscape to its usual
bustle, and the hovering soul
waiting to be born, to take on
its shadow? Everything rests

on the rooster's desire
for the sun, old sweetheart.
He must close his eyes to resume
his passionate crowing.

THE STATE OF THE WORLD

The world has been sad since
Tuesday, but dutifully performs
her punctual illuminations.
After the heavings and mammalian
incantations, why doesn't she
give it a rest, go slack and blank
like an overweight Maja who has been
royally fucked? Watch the faithless
lover slither off with skin
between his teeth.

★

Hunter, the old arthritic German
shorthaired pointer, knocked over
the garbage again. Ants flock
to last night's dinner, lamb riblets,
with a sense of purpose
rivaling pilgrims.

★

Gaidar Aliadev, sous-chef, chef, now
high-ranking member of Russia's politburo,
clawed his way out of the slime by back-
biting, blackmailing, asslicking patrons.
The newspapers call him progressive.

★

And the world sighs, shifts a haunch,
realigns her motionless center

where the trapped moment risks nothing
and subsides. The clouds, having been
hauled out in advance, are more careful
in their formations. Even so,
there is a ramshackle hut where
even now the table is set.

BORDER DISPATCH

In a remote district an old man
consoles himself with pornographic
photos, enraptured by animal acts
he no longer performs. Just as

the acne-scarred motorcycle mechanic
slicks his eye over the road and takes
time with tools. Precision is slow work,

a young girl picking a scab off her knee
but sparing the layer of pale pink skin.
This is what happens when rollerskates

travel faster than the body lagging
behind like a spent bloodhound
who fails to keep pace with the fox.

                    ★

A woman fastening her dress
studies the form
sprawled on the bed.
Men come, she thinks,
to sleep, to abandon
themselves to sleep.
The young ones
curl up like puppies
protecting their soft parts.
She inspects the contents
of his wallet, removes

a tenspot, applies
fresh lipstick in the dark.

★

The early light of morning is
impartial, leaf rot, the black
ribs of trees as indistinct as
the moral nature of the world,
the way we graduate from symbol
to the infinitesimal. Now
we are nameless, now without
income. Somewhere a window
opens and an arm extends, palm
up as if in supplication. What
will fall from the sky today?

THE FUTURE HAS ALREADY HAPPENED

Imagine I'm little red riding hood
and you're the woodcutter and you've
read it too. Imagine the wild Caesarean,
the ax and its fresh cut, the blade
running deep. And me springing out
to dance on the planked floor with Granny
in her white nightdress, soft and white
to the touch. Oh the body and its sweet
decay! But I leap ahead of the story.
Years later we meet and we marry,
then there's the birthing and the baking
of cookies to be carried in a basket
by the girl setting out in her red hood.

Books from Dryad Press

Roger Aplon, *By Dawn's Early Light at 120 Miles Per Hour;*
 Stiletto
Denis Boyles, *Maxine's Flattery*
Ann Darr, *Cleared for Landing*
Frank Dwyer, *Looking Wayward*
Roland Flint, *And Morning;* *Say It
Barbara Goldberg, *Cautionary Tales*
Jack Greer, *America and Other Poems*
Marguerite Harris, ed., *A Tumult for John Berryman*
Slavko Janevski, *The Bandit Wind* (translated by Charles Simic)
Philip K. Jason, *Thawing Out; Near the Fire;*
 Shaping: New Poems in Traditional Prosodies (editor)
Rod Jellema, *The Lost Faces;* *The Eighth Day: New &*
 Selected Poems
Rodger Kamenetz, *Nympholepsy; The Missing Jew*
Barbara Lefcowitz, *The Wild Piano*
Merrill Leffler, *Partly Pandemonium, Partly Love*
Neil Lehrman, *Perdut (a novel)*
John Logan, *Poem in Progress*
Linda Pastan, *On the Way to the Zoo;* *Setting the Table*
Harry Rand, trans., *The Beginning of Things*
John Russell, *Honey Russell: Between Games, Between Halves*
Myra Sklarew, *From the Backyard of the Diaspora*
Susan Sonde, *Inland is Parenthetical*
Sidney Sulkin, *The Secret Seed: Stories & Poems*
Herman Taube, *Between the Shadows: New & Selected Works*
Reed Whittemore, *The Feel of Rock: Poems of Three Decades*
Irving Wilner, *Poems of the Later Years*
James Wright, *Moments of the Italian Summer* *
Paul Zimmer, *The Zimmer Poems;* *With Wanda: Town &*
 Country Poems

* No longer in print